GIVE GOD THE PRAISE!

Whatever He Does, Wherever You are

Miracles and Poems

MaryL

ISBN 979-8-88644-410-0 (Paperback)
ISBN 979-8-88644-411-7 (Digital)

Covenant Books
11661 Hwy 707
Murrells Inlet, SC 29576
www.covenantbooks.com

ALWAYS GIVE GOD THE PRAISE FOR HIS MIGHTY MIRACLES

I've always loved to tell stories and write poems, and so did my mother, Fay Elizabeth Jeffers. In her memory, I'm putting a verse from Psalms with all the miracles I write about. The book of Psalms was mother's favorite.

Mother loved to read the book of Psalms. After my dad died, my husband and I stayed all night with her. She wanted to read Psalms. She read a few verses, I read some, and so did my husband. I think we read the whole book before we went to bed.

Miracles still happen today.

Chapter 1

MOTHER'S SALVATION

The first miracle that happened in my life happened before I was born.

It was when my oldest sister was a baby. I don't know how old she was, but for some reason, she stopped breathing. Grandma (on my dad's side) picked her up and walked the floor praying, and life came back into her little body.

Mother told me that was when she gave her life to Christ. She raised us children to love and fear God. Mother didn't have anything but the necessities of life, but she would feed anyone who came to our house, even if it was just pinto beans, biscuits, and gravy. She was known for her biscuits.

Wow! That miracle set the path of our lives as a family. The miracle story and Christian example was then passed down to our generation and, hopefully, on to the next generations until Jesus comes to take us all home.

> My mouth shall speak the praise of
> the Lord: and let all flesh bless His
> holy name for ever and ever.
> —Psalm 145:21

{ *I See God* }

Flowers all around, with shades of pink, purples, and blues.
Trees with their branches that spread,
with leaves in deep green hues.
The water that reaches out in its vastness, as if it touches the sky.
I view it all and marvel at the breathtaking beauty; with joy, I sigh.
God is all around us as he paints a wonderful view.
He wants his children to be happy—that is me and also you.
He finishes every picture with traces of enduring love.
This is the way our Father is as he looks down from above.
Puts a circle of protection around us. If we open our eyes, we'll see.
His love is showing through every tree.
O God, our Father in heaven. Oh, how I praise you when I pray!
Open my heart to see you and the beginning of each new day.

Chapter 2

MY BIG BROTHER

Every girl needs a big brother, especially one like mine. He was very shy and stuttered a little when excited. He had a beautiful smile and a pleasant personality. His name was Neal. As I write this, I have just lost him at the age of seventy-seven. I will miss him here on earth, but I will see him again someday in heaven.

We lived on the Starrett Farm by the Kanawha River in West Virginia. I was a real tomboy. I'd go out adventuring and fall out of trees, and grapevines broke while I was swinging on them. I had the breath knocked out of me more times than I can remember. It was Neal who carried me home many times with my cuts and bruises.

God provided a brother to save my life the day I stepped into an underground spring at the edge of the river. It was quicksand that pulled me in up to my waist. Neal climbed up a tree (*that God planted in that very spot where the spring was*), and he pulled me out. This was a real struggle because it was pulling me in! I was twelve, and Neal was fourteen.

He has been a good example to me and all our peers, as well as others. He lived his life as an example, telling others about Jesus.

O give thanks unto the Lord: for He is
good: for His mercy endureth forever.
—Psalm 136:1

The Woods of Life

As I walk through the woods of life,
I see all the miracles that God has put before me.
I want to walk slowly, tune in love, and feel no strife.
The beautiful sky, pale blue with clouds of white, I see.
The shapes will only stay for a moment or so.
Was that a bird I heard behind a tree?
The clouds scatter in the sky as the wind starts to blow.
The trees make a sound that startles me.
The leaves wave in the wind and wave goodbye to the day.
The day moves on as the sun goes down.
Thank God for His Son and all that He has given, I pray.
There is a smile on my face, no need for a frown.
This world can be sad, but we have Jesus to dry our eyes.
Now the color changes from blue to hues of red and gold.
He changes the mood of our heart as the sun sets in the sky.
As it hides its face in warm colors of God's rainbow of old.
It's now time to lay down the labor of our hands,
To spend time and relax and have family time.
As I look in the dark sky of life, I thank God for friends.
As the stars start to twinkle, it's like singing a rhyme.
It's time to thank God for the day and all that He's given.
The moon starts to shine and light up the sky.
Jesus, I thank You for the cross and Your side that was riven.
I think of His mercy as I end the day with a sigh.
Then I shut my eyes and let God handle tomorrow.

Chapter 3

1965 CAR ACCIDENT

A week before my wedding day, my fiancé, Lloyd, and I were going to the apartment where he was staying to take some veggies from his aunt Ethel's garden and other things we would need to start housekeeping. We were going to live there for a while after we got married.

We were on the way to Linwood Avenue in Columbus, Ohio. We were in his Volkswagen, traveling north on Elm Creek Drive. All of a sudden, on Williams Road, a car ran a stop sign, and we crashed into it. After he had become conscious, Lloyd pulled me out of the car because it was smoking. When I opened my eyes, I was in the middle of the road with fire trucks and emergency vehicles with lights flashing. A young man (the person that hit us) was on his knees praying for me.

I went to the hospital with bruises and a large cut on my leg. I later found out that my spine had been misaligned. I had to have therapy to straighten it for several years.

In spite of the accident, I limped down the aisle the next Saturday and got married. I found out the miracle of this story twenty years later.

My lower back started hurting, and the doctor x-rayed it and asked, "When did you break your back?" I told him I didn't know

that I had. He told me it had been broken all the way across my tail-
bone. Then he said, "Oh well. It healed well."

God healed it the day of the accident.

> He brought me up also out of a horrible
> pit, out of the miry clay, and set my feet
> upon a rock and established my goings.
> —Psalm 40:2

Not My Will But Thine

My Will Is To Have Riches And Fame;
Thy Will Is For Me To Serve You.
My Will Is To Please Self (the flesh);
Thy Will Is To Humble Myself Before You.
My Will Is To Be Thought Of Well;
Thy Will Is To Do Good In Secret.
My Will Is To Judge My Neighbor;
Thy Will Is To Judge Myself.
My Will Is To Look At The World;
Thy Will Is To Look At The Cross.
My Will Is To Have Salvation Without Obedience;
Thy Will Is To Tell Others About The Savior.
My Will Is To Be Strong-Willed And Stubborn;
Thy Will Is To Be Broken Daily.
My Will Is To Want; Thy Will Is to Give.
My Will Is To Live;
Thy Will Was To Die For Me.

Chapter 4

THE NIGHT I CRIED UNTO THE LORD

I grew up in church and heard all the stories in the Bible. Then one day when I was seventeen, I was convicted in my heart, and I went forward in church. I shook hands with the preacher and told him I wanted to be saved. He sprinkled me on the head, and I joined the church.

I didn't understand what I was doing. I thought that was all I had to do to be saved. I started teaching Sunday school but never led anyone to the Lord. I didn't know how.

I got married when I was twenty-one, and we were married nine months before my husband, Lloyd, was drafted into the army. When I found out he was going to Vietnam, I quit my job in Columbus and moved in with Lloyd's parents. They lived in the country in West Virginia.

I stayed in Lloyd's childhood room in an old farmhouse. His parents farmed the land, and so they went to bed at seven o'clock every night and got up early the next day. It was dark in that room, and the stairs squeaked and creaked at night. I was so scared in that house. I was struggling, convinced that Lloyd wasn't going to make it home. He was in search and destroy—that was the worst job ever.

One night in my room, I started to cry. I couldn't take it anymore. I called out to God and said, "Where are you? I need you right now."

He directed me to the top of the TV. There was a small salvation tract on it that my mother-in-law had put there. It told me I was a sinner and needed a Savior and what to do about it. I then asked God to forgive me for my sins, and I asked Jesus to come into my heart and save my soul. He did and He gave me a peace, and I knew that Lloyd would come home all right.

Now, fifty-five years later, I have Lloyd, one son (John), four grandchildren (Nathan, Kaytlin, Caleb, and Kylee), and one great-grandson (Wyatt). Praise the Lord!

> I sought the Lord, and he heard me
> and delivered me from all my fears.
>
> —Psalm 34: 41

Peace and Understanding

I met Him on a farm, in the spring,
His gentle hand held mine as He whispered, "I love you."
He gave me peace and understanding of what love was all about.
He carried me through the hard times and
dried the tears from my eyes.
He gave me peace and understanding of what life was all about.
Upon the return of the man I love, He showed me compassion.
He made me see happy times in the eyes of the one I love.
He gave me peace and understanding,
knowing I could trust in Him.
His name is Jesus, and He gave His life for me.

Chapter 5

THE RABID DOG

In 1967, my husband was in Vietnam. His job was search and destroy deep in the jungle.

After being there for a few months, he was bit by a rabid dog on a landing zone and had to go back to base camp for the shots. While he was taking the shots at base camp, his entire squadron was overtaken and killed.

God took him out of the free-fire zone to protect him. His mother, the church back home, and I had been earnestly praying for his health and protection. This is just one of the many miracles that God performed while he was there.

And all men shall fear, and shall
declare the work of God: for they shall
wisely consider of His doing.

—Psalm 64:9

The Autumn of Your Life

As you walk through the autumn of your life,
I pray your life will be bright like the golden and
Red leaves of the fall trees.
Sometimes the leaves will crunch under your feet,
The wind will blow,
A leaf will fall and brush against your cheek.
Then there will be days the frost will come with its bite,
Nipping at your nose.
God will be there to warm you as you walk along life's pathway.
He will lift your spirit and calm your heart as long as you
Love one another and trust in Him.
There will be no fear of the deep snow that will come
Because His love will be there to comfort and strengthen
You in all of life's niches.
When the time comes (hopefully, the rapture) and we
Will all be in heaven, it will be worth it all.
The snow will be gone, and the cold breeze will never, ever
Give us a chill again.
What a day of rejoicing that will be!

Chapter 6

A WARNING

My husband, Lloyd, and I were coming home from West Virginia after visiting our parents. It had already gotten dark. Lloyd had gotten very sleepy, so I said, "Let me drive." (I always say that the first miracle was he said that I could drive.) Most of the time, he says, "No, that's okay."

As I was driving along, I heard a voice in my head. It said, "Car passing!"

I thought, "Where?" I kept looking around when, all of a sudden, there were headlights coming toward me on my side of the road.

I pulled over into the berm and let it pass. It was bumpy on the berm. Lloyd woke up startled and said, "It looked like that car was on our side of the road."

I said, "Tell me about it!"

If I hadn't been warned, I might have hit that car head-on. But God gave me a warning that caused me to be prepared for it.

I wonder how many times God gives us warnings that we don't heed.

I'm sure glad I did.

> I will sing unto the Lord, because He
> hath dealt bountifully with me.
> —Psalm 13:6

Listen to God's Calling

I sat down on a rock and watched a monarch
butterfly as it fluttered from place to place.
It would set for a moment then fly again to
another place, from a flower to a rock.
I began to wonder. What was it thinking, or did
it even think? Did it go as God directed?
That is what we should do. God as God directs.
When we spend too much time thinking, fear
and doubt step in.
Maybe if God wants us to go and talk to some-
one about Him, we start to think that they
won't listen or it might offend them.
If we would only do as God directs, our lives
would be more blessed.
The Bible says He will be with us, even to the
end of the world.
That is His promise. So instead of thinking
foolishly,
Listen to God's calling. Pray and go!

Chapter 7

GOD'S ANGELS

When my son, John, was still in a walker, I went into the kitchen to get a drink. I felt he was perfectly safe in the walker because it was only a few steps away. I turned around, and he was gone!

I looked at the back door. It was open to the landing at the top of the stairs leading to the basement (*instant shock*). I ran to the door and onto the landing just in time to see him go all the way to the basement in the air!

I could not think. I just held my breath. He never touched one step. When the walker hit the floor of the basement, it was still on its rollers. He was in the air the whole time.

I ran down the stairs. John gave a big scream. I checked him out. He didn't even have a bump on his head. He was scared but not hurt—riding on angels' wings.

The basement door must not have been all the way shut, and he somehow managed to open it.

I thank God for his protection.

> The angel of the Lord encampeth round about
> them that fear Him, and delivers them.
> —Psalm 34:7

Hope

Hope is what everyone wants.
Trust is what we all need.
Without trust, there is no hope.
Without hope, all is doomed.
But when we put our trust in
the solid rock of Jesus Christ,
there is hope.
He is the rock we stand on.
Wait on His love to perform its miracles.
God's love carries us through
The valleys, over the hills, and
through the rivers of danger.
We have hope—Jesus!

Chapter 8

JOHN'S STORY

My son, John, was drafted into the army and was stationed in Fort Belvoir, Virginia. He called one evening and said he was coming home for the weekend and would be home at four o'clock in the morning.

My husband and I decided we would stay up to wait for him because we both knew he had fallen asleep while driving at night before. About two o'clock in the morning, I said to Lloyd, "Let's go pray for him. I feel like he is in danger." I prayed that God would send an angel to keep him awake.

He arrived home at four in the morning like he said he would. We gave each other hugs and thanked God he was home. I explained to him how I had gotten worried and said we needed to pray for him and that I had asked God to send an angel to keep him awake.

He said, "So that's what that was! What time was that?"

I said, "Two a.m."

He explained that he had been okay for a while, but then he started to doze off. He woke up, and it looked like a man was sitting beside him in the car! He looked at the clock, and it was two a.m. He said, "I blew it off, thinking it was a dream. Then I started to doze again, and there was a man sitting beside me again! Then I stopped the car, got out, and looked around."

I'm not sure what good that would do since the car had been rolling. How could someone have gotten inside?

John continued, "I saw nothing. I got back in the car, and I was so scared that I didn't doze anymore."

> My soul fainteth for thy salvation:
> but I hope in thy word.
> —Psalm 119:81

Stop and Share

Big brown eyes I did see.
Full of sorrow, she looked at me
as she sat on a wagon by a tree.
I looked inside them, sad as can be.
Who is the little girl by the tree?
To whom does she belong? I don't know.
She sat there watching as I did go.
Not a smile did she give, no sign of a glow.
Those big brown eyes, a tear did flow.
What was the matter, I'll never know.
I walked on by on my way there.
Those eyes, they haunted me. I whispered a prayer
For the little girl hugging her teddy bear.
"Lord, will you help her in your tender care?"
Oh, not for a minute did Jesus I share.

Many years have now gone by.
She is still in my prayers as I cry.
Jesus, save her and take her on high.
That little girl with a tear in her eye.
A peace says I will meet her someday in the sky.

Chapter 9

CALEB'S SALVATION

My grandchildren would take turns staying all night at my house. Now it was Caleb's turn. He was six years old. When we got into the car, he started to sing, "I'm going to Mamau's house! I going to Mamau's house!" Then he stopped to say, "Mamau, do you know what I'm going to do when I get to your house?"

I said, "No, what?"

He said, "I'm going to get saved."

I said, "Great!"

Then we did our usual things when the grandchildren spent the night. We went to the dollar store, out to lunch, and then back to my house.

We got back to my house, and I proceeded to unload the car and put things away. He ran into the living room and said, "Mamau, did you forget what I was going to do?"

I hurried into the living room, where I kept a little altar for the children to pray. I explained to him about salvation, what it all meant, and what to say to God to get saved. He started to pray, "Dear God, forgive me for my sin, and help me to serve you. I want to be your child and go to heaven. Help me not to lie and get in fights with Katie and Nathan and obey Mommy and Daddy. In Jesus's name, amen."

Then he looked up out the window and said woefully, "O Lord, I forgot to ask you to come in my heart." Then he bowed his head and said, "Jesus, would you come into my heart and save me? Amen."

> And whosoever you shall ask in my
> name, that will I do, that the Father
> may be glorified in the son.
> —John 14:13

The Time Is Almost Here

I can almost hear the feet of Jesus coming in the sky.
As he prepares the earth for its final goodbye.
This world is becoming more evil as the days go by.
Man is disobeying God with the evil's great big lie.
The devil is shouting louder with his battle cry.
God is trying to tell us not to listen in his evil craze.
Some are not listening and not giving Him praise.
They are falling in filth of sin in many, many ways.
Maybe there is not much time and hours or maybe days.
Lift your eyes, children. God will make us anew.
He wants you to praise Him, and He will get you through.
Look to heaven, and you will see what He wants you to do.
Keep trusting in our God in heaven, and
He will take away the blue.

Chapter 10

DOG AT THE BACK DOOR

Every so often, Lloyd would be sent out of town for a job. On one job, he was gone for three days. The first day he was gone, I heard a scratching and whining at the patio door. I looked out. It was a big dog. Since I was afraid of big dogs that I didn't know, I ignored him. I did see him playing with the neighbor kids, but that didn't make me feel any better about him.

But every night, he would sleep on my patio, against the door. The only time I would go outside, I would go to the car in the garage and get inside then open the door. Same thing when I came home. But every night, he would be there, like he was at home on my patio.

The day Lloyd was coming home, I called the dogcatcher and told him there was a dog hanging around my house, and I was afraid of him. He came and tried to get the dog, but it would growl at him.

The man asked if I could come out and call him. When I did, he wagged his tail and came toward me! I ran into the garage, and he followed. Then the man caught him and put a leash around his neck. The dog looked at me and whined like I did him a dirty deal. Then the dogcatcher took him away.

I felt the man might have thought I was the owner and just wanted to get rid of him. But later, I thought maybe God sent him to guard the house while Lloyd was gone. Maybe there was a reason for him being there.

> And the Lord shall help them, and deliver
> them: he shall deliver them from the wicked
> and save them because they trust in Him.
> —Psalm 37:40

Don't Let the Qualms Get You Down

Qualms roam around in your head,
They make you wish you were dead.
They tell you lies, confuse your mind.
They don't want you to be kind.
They are not sent by God above,
They are not sent out of love.
You wish and wonder from where they came.
You become anxious, sad, and lame.
They are negative thoughts that enter your brain.
You pray to God that you won't go insane.
Start to sing praises to His holy name.
In the Lord I put my trust.
Praise Him, thank Him—that's a must.

Chapter 11

SHANNON ROAD EXPERIENCE

Lloyd was out of town. I was coming home from our church. I got to the crossroads of Shannon and Gender Road, where there was a stop sign. As I stopped, I looked across Shannon Road and saw a car stop at the opposite stop sign from me. I looked to my left, and I saw a pickup truck coming down Gender Road.

Then I had a strange feeling. I felt the car was going to pull out and the truck was going to hit it. So I backed up and waited. The car did pull out, and the truck did hit it! The truck knocked that car clear down Gender Road.

I got out of my car and walked toward the truck. The man got out of the truck on the other side, kind of stunned. But the woman on the passenger side of the truck couldn't get her seat belt off, so I helped her. It kind of hurt her stomach.

I think the police came and directed traffic away, so I left at that time. I don't know what happened to the people in the car, but what I am sure of is that God let me know so I would not be in that horrible accident.

The earth is the Lord's and the fullness thereof,
the world and they that dwell therein.
—Psalm 24:1

The Water of Life

Today I was sitting, looking out the window.
A goldfinch lit on the hummingbird feeder.
He sat there as the wind blew him back and forth.
He picked at the top. He looked around and at the
Sweet water in the bottle, but he didn't know how
To get to it.
He kept on swinging in the wind and picking at the
Top of the feeder.
The gold on his body reminded me of the streets
　of gold.
The black on his body reminded me of our sin.
It reminded me of the humans who come to see
　the water but don't know how to get to it.
They swing around and look at the world, enjoy-
　ing the swinging.
But they don't have anyone to tell them how to
　get to the water of life.
We have the answer.
Don't neglect to tell the searching one how to get
　to the Son of the Living Water.

Chapter 12

LITTLE BIRD

L loyd was out of town again. We were having a sunroom built at the back of our house. It had all the windows in it but no door yet.

One day, I was outside and looked in, and there was a little bird flying against the windows. It would fall, get back up, and try to get out again. After a while, it stopped on the windowsill and was breathing hard. I'm sure it was hurting.

I walked over to the window and said, "Little bird, God loves you, and so do I. And if you will hop on my finger, I will take you to safety." I held out my finger, and the little bird hopped on it.

I thought, *No one will believe what just happened.* So I put my hand over it and took it out front, where my daughter-in-law and my grandchildren were.

I told them the story. I said, "Here is the little bird!" I took my hand off it. Then I said, "Okay, little bird, you can fly away now." And it flew up into the sky. It let me put my hand over it and sat peacefully until I let it go.

God must have told it I was okay and he could trust me.

> For God is King of all the earth; sing
> ye praises with understanding.
> —Psalm 47:7

Our Life with Jesus

When we live our life with Jesus and travel along the way,
He will keep you and comfort you as we kneel to pray.
In the beginning, He gives you birth,
We grow in body upon this earth.
As we grow older, burdens we bear.
Look to God; He really does care.
The peace He gives you beyond your pain.
Seek Him daily; it won't be in vain.
Our loved ones are here, just for a season.
They are taken from us; God knows the reason.
So look for Him in the garden green,
Where the flowers bloom and the birds sing.
Ask Him today to come into your heart,
And today there will be a brand-new start.
Loved ones are waiting for you to come too.
Accept Jesus today, and He will see you through.

Chapter 13

GOD HAS A REASON

I was out shopping and stopped at the card rack because my brother Neal's birthday was coming up on December 25.

I started a conversation with a woman who was also looking. I told her when my brother's birthday was. At first, I made small talk and was complaining about how a person could only find a spiritual card in a Christian bookstore.

Then I came to myself and began talking about God and how He sent His Son to die on the cross for us so we could have a home in heaven.

Then I continued talking about my brothers and how I had five of them. You know, silly conversations about how brothers are. I said, "Well, you know what I'm talking about. Wait. How could you, since you only have two sisters?"

She looked at me, shocked, and asked, "How do you know that?"

I said, "I don't know."

I walked out of the store in shock. We were strangers! How did I know?

I came home thinking about it. I told my husband about it that evening. He pointed out, "Maybe she had to have confirmation that what you said was true about the Bible. So God gave you a knowing."

Should we always, as Christians, be surprised when God does something that is mysterious?

> I will cry unto the Lord most high: unto
> God that performeth all things for me.
> —Psalm 57:2

The Rose

As I look out my window this morning,
I see red roses blowing in the wind.
Bowing with petals soft and humble
Then rising again in their true beauty.
They remind me of the scarlet blood of Jesus
That was shed on the cross for me.
On them are the thorns that were on His head
As He suffered.
Behind the roses are purple flowers that claim
His royal blood.
A yellow goldfinch lands on the rose,
Reminding me of the streets of heaven.
The green bush behind tells me to grow in grace.
It won't be long until the Rose of Sharon
Returns again.
Another form of the Rose blooming again: Jesus.

Chapter 14

THE LADY IN THE WOODS

My husband and I moved to a different neighborhood. Many times, as I was exploring, I saw a lady walking down a long lane. I would see her once in a while as I went by and would wave to her as I passed.

She was a nice lady. I would stop by sometimes to have a conversation with her. One day, I found out her husband had died and she was alone. I felt so bad for her because she had no children to care for her. That inspired me to talk to her even more. As the years went by, I talked to her, and we became friends.

Then one day, I was passing out invitations to an Easter program happening in our church. She had told me that she was of a different religion, so I wasn't sure how she would accept the flyer.

I greeted her, and she said, "Isn't growing old for the birds?"

I responded, "Yes, I guess it is."

Then she said, "But it's better than the alternative."

Man, how God works! The door was open for me to say, "If the alternative happens, do you know where you would go?"

She replied, "No, I don't."

I said, "Would you like to? I can tell you if you would let me."

She said, "Yes, I would."

So I proceed to tell her how she could go to heaven. She listened, accepted Jesus as her Savior, and is now a sister in Christ!

During the pandemic, we continued to talk to each other on the phone. Now we will be friends for life and after.

The Lord is my light and my salvation:
whom shall I fear? The Lord is the strength
of my life; of whom shall I be afraid.
—Psalm 27:1

It's Going to Be a Mighty Fine Day

I woke up this morning and went to the window. The sun's rays were shining through. It looked like liquid gold pouring through the room.

I said to myself, "Thank you, God. It's going to be a mighty fine day.

"Today I'm going to watch my two-year-old great-grandson. We always have a good day."

My grandson came, and when he sat Wyatt down, he ran to me with a big smile on his face. I picked him up and gave him a big kiss.

When he said his goodbyes to his daddy, he turned around and said, "The room." That was his playroom. He started hitting and kicking balloons that I had left over from a recent party.

Next came the plastic bottles that I had stacked like pyramids around the room. We pretended we were knocking down the walls of Jericho.

Now it was breakfast time. I put him in his chair, and he folded his little hands and waited for me to bless the food. When I finished, he said, "A-man."

He ate his food, and when he was done, he was done. You couldn't coax him to take another bite. Same with coloring, reading a book, and so on.

Now we played with cars on the floor. That silly
car bumped into something. He giggled.
I got a new cartoon movie about the birth of
Jesus. He didn't watch much of it, but I'm
anxious to see how soon he understands.
When his dad came to pick him up, he kissed me
goodbye and said he loved me.
Yes, it was a mighty fine day.

Chapter 15

DIAMOND RING

One day, I came home from somewhere and went to the bedroom. I started to take off my engagement ring and put it away. It was kind of stuck, so I pulled again. It fell to the floor, and I got down to search for it. There wasn't anything on the floor. I prayed that God would help me find it.

Every day, I looked for it. I told a friend about my struggle. She had a metal finder and brought it over to help me. We searched and searched and never found it. I prayed again that God would show me where it was.

A year later, I opened the door in my dresser and pulled out the top drawer to grab my purple socks. As I was putting them on, I felt a pebble in the toe. I felt around to seize it. As I caught it, I thought, *It can't be!*

But there it was, my diamond ring. How it got there, God only knows.

A friend said that God preserved it for me in royalty (the purple sock in the highest drawer in the dresser) while it was lost.

Be thou exalted, O God, above the Heavens:
let thy glory be above all the earth.
—Psalm 57: 11

Color

Without light, there is abstinence of color.
You learn as you grow from a child to a scholar.
It's God's gift to us from the day of birth.
He made pretty trees to fill the earth.
Mountains of pink, blue, and purple in the scape,
Dotted with snow to continue the scene.
Skies of blue, grass that is green, the prettiest
Flowers you've ever seen.
They all bring happiness to our lives; see the look
On a child's face
When a pretty flower he does embrace.
Look what He made for us to enjoy.
Sunsets of orange, yellow, and pink—it's there to
Brighten your day
As you travel along God's pathway.
Look around you, and color you will see.
The miracles of God on the deep blue sea.
See God's power through the universe display.
Praise Him today, and thank Him as you pray.
O God, I thank you for what you have done,
Especially for sending your wonderful Son.

Chapter 16

TEN-YEAR-OLD GIRL

I have taught Sunday school for fifty years, and I never know what is going to happen.

One day, a little girl named G'avonie was in my class. She was really disruptive in class. I told her, "If you act up next Sunday the way you did this Sunday, you will have to go into the hallway and sit with my helper during class so everyone else won't be disturbed!"

She didn't show up the next Sunday. I felt like I blew it. I kept worrying about it, so I prayed. I prayed that she would come back and would come into my classroom before anyone else came. As I prayed, the Lord impressed upon my heart to buy her a cross pendant.

I was preparing my lesson early the next Sunday. She came to the door hesitantly. I invited her in. She sat down, and I told her I had something for her. I took the little cross out of the box and put it around her neck and said, "I want you to wear this and remember that Jesus loves you, and so do I. He died on the cross for you so you can go to heaven."

She smiled and said thank-you. By that time, the other children started to come in. She got up and left with them for opening exercises.

I thought about it later. She always came on the church bus. How did she get there early? Who brought her?

When Sunday school started, the girls came in and sat down. I prayed and proceeded to teach the lesson. She was really good that day. She listened to every word.

After everyone left, she stayed and said, "I want to know how to get to heaven."

I explained to her how everyone was a sinner after the first man (Adam and Eve) sinned in the garden. Then we were born in sin, and we needed a Savior. So God sent His only Son to be born and to die and shed His blood for our sins. Then He rose again from the grave and went back to heaven. If you ask Him to forgive you and ask Him to come into your heart and save you, He will if you are serious about it.

Then she bowed her head and accepted Jesus as her Savior.

The next Sunday, she came back to class and listened. After the lesson, she asked me if she could write something on the board. I told her, "Okay, if it is nothing bad." She said it wasn't.

She wrote, "If anyone in here would like to have Jesus in their heart and get saved from that awful place, talk to our teacher."

That day, four girls stayed and accepted Jesus as their Savior.

I talked to the bus captain, and she noted that something had changed about G'avonie. She had been behaving very well on the bus.

I told her what had happened, and we gave God the praise.

> O God, thou art my God: early will I
> seek thee: my soul thirsteth for thee,
> my flesh longeth for thee in a dry and
> thirsty land, where there is no water.
> —Psalm 63:1

What Kind of Vessel Are We?

A vessel that sits on a shelf with pride
When the pain is more than we can hide.
It displays its beauty every day.
Does it stop to kneel and pray?
It has cracks. Does anyone care?
Examine this vessel and be aware
Of what God has for you.
He can mend those cracks and pull
You through.
When our hearts are full of pain,
Run to Jesus. His love you will gain.

Chapter 17

THE MAN CALLED SCOTT

In my little town, we had a grocery store that I went to frequently. There was a man in his sixties who would always greet everyone with a smile and say, "Hi, how are you today?"

I would say, "I'm fine. How are you?" Then I would proceed with my shopping.

Then one day, I came into the store, and as usual, he said, "Hi, how are you?"

I answered the usual then looked him in the eyes and said, "But how are you?"

He said, "Not so good. I've been diagnosed with stage 4 cancer."

I proceeded to say, "I'm so sorry. Tell me your first name, and I will pray for you."

He said, "Scott."

After that, I not only prayed for God to heal him but also for his salvation. When I would go in the store after that, he would update me on his progress—new medicine and whatever.

Then about a month later, I saw him in the store aisle on his knees, stocking the shelves. I asked, "How are you doing?"

He said, "I don't think I'm going to make it."

The Lord impressed upon me to ask him, "If you don't make it, do you know where you are going if you would pass away?"

He said, "No, I don't."

So I proceeded to tell him what he had to do.

While he was on his knees, he accepted the Lord as his Savior. He got up gloriously saved!

I didn't see him again. Then three weeks later, I saw a note on the door of the grocery store. It said Scott had passed away.

I asked myself, "What if I hadn't obeyed the Lord and responded to his call?"

> In God is my salvation and my glory: the rock
> of my strength and my refuge is in God.
> —Psalm 62:7

My life is
Like a roller-coaster ride.
I fear and doubt, worry and hide.
I turn to Jesus and surrender my pride.
Way down deep in the depths of me,
My heart starts to sing the joy of Thee.
It starts to raise up to the sky
When I talk
To the Lord on high.
It starts to sing down
As I ask Him to forgive my sin.
My soul makes an upward bound
As I sing His praises with
A heavenly sound.
The Spirit beckons me. I rejoice
In His love. You see me; my soul cries out.
Up again, back to heaven, joy within! I long
For You, Almighty God! Inside I tremble, tears
Start to flow. I know you are with me wherever
I go. My spirit soars with unknown love for the
Savior that looks down from above. My meek
Little soul, You died for me. I'll be waiting
When You come back again to take me
To heaven, where I'll be
Free from sin.

Thank you again, Jesus,
For dying for me. A place called
Heaven is where I'll be. Singing
Praises to His holy name, my soul
Takes a leap up again. I'm not worthy.
But I will say You did it anyway.
You cleansed me within with Your
Shed blood. You freely gave so I
And my family could be saved.

Chapter 18

GOD LEADS

One day, I went to church extra early. I went into my classroom and prepared my Sunday-school lesson. I walked into the sanctuary, and a young lady came in. I started a conversation with her. In the conversation, she started telling me that she had been diagnosed with cancer, that she had two sons, and that she had kicked her boyfriend out of her house and wanted to make things right.

Then God laid it on my heart to say, "Let's go to my classroom, where we can talk in private."

We sat down, and she began to ask questions about religion and what she had been taught. I explained some things to her about the differences between her religion and Christianity. God laid on my heart to read her John 14. After I read it, she said, "Wow! How could something written so long ago pertain to me now?"

I told her it wasn't written for just the people of long ago. God is for all times.

After we talked for a while, she said, "You will have to tell me what to say to become a child of God."

I said, "I can tell you. But whatever you say, you have to believe it and mean it in your heart."

She prayed and now Jesus was her Savior. She didn't stay for the services after that because she wasn't feeling well, but she received what she had come for.

I tried to see her again, but she was too sick. She moved and I never heard from her again. I don't know where she is or if God healed her or not, but whether she survived the cancer or not, she is or will be in heaven someday.

> Trust in Him at all times: ye people,
> pour out your heart before Him.
> God is a refuge for us. Shelah.
> —Psalm 62:8

You Are There, O God

Thou art the Most High, holy God.
I look to the hills, you are there.
The soft breeze blowing, you whisper.
I look to the sea, you are there.
As I walk alone in this world, without a friend,
I look to the sky, you are there.
I see a glimpse of a shadow; I feel your presence.
My heart sings with joy, you are there.
I know how precious thou are, thy majesty,
My God, my hope—you are there.
Problems of this world consume me,
I feel my breath is about to go.
Then I look up and see your face.
You are here.

Chapter 19

DEER CROSSING

My husband and I were going to West Virginia to visit our parents. We always prayed for God to protect us before traveling.

After driving for about an hour, it got so dark. All of a sudden, there was a deer! We didn't see it until it was a foot in front of our bumper, but it never got any closer. I watched as it passed in front of our car then moved on to the other side. We watched as it ran away. It was a ten-pointer and very large!

I exclaimed to my husband, "That was a miracle!"

He said, "Yes, I know! I was beside myself! The car was going sixty-five miles per hour, and we didn't get any closer!"

God must have sent an angel to hold the car back.

God takes care of His children. He is always close.

Many, O Lord my God, are the wonderful
works which thou hast done, and thy
thoughts which are to us-ward they cannot
be reckoned up in order unto thee: If I
would declare and speak of them, they
are more than can be numbered.

—Psalm 40:5

Today I woke up with birds singing a song of joy
as a mockingbird flew on my windowsill.
It had just rained, and water droplets were on the window.
As the sun shone through, it made tiny prisms on the windowsill.
I pulled back the curtain, and the bird flew away in second or so.
I saw it soar up into the pale blue sky with fluffy white clouds.
I marveled with a sigh.
I looked across the yard.
Beyond the trees, three deer scampered with
white tails bouncing along behind.
Then they were gone in a flash. I waved goodbye.
Oh, what heaven must be! It must be a sign.
The flowers were blooming. I stood and
pondered God's mighty creation.
The first glimpse of Jesus, too much to unfold.
The singing of the angels—O what heaven must be!
The shine in the city and from the streets of gold.
Our loved ones who have gone on before, no death, no sin.
Wow, it makes me want to shout.
It will always be spring in heaven, no doubt.

Chapter 20

CATHY'S STORY

I went to visit a nursing home with some ladies from my church. We talked to some people and gave gifts to some. Then we went into a room where there was a woman lying on a mattress on the floor.

They said that she couldn't communicate with us, but my friend Cathy wasn't going to let it go. She lay down on the mattress with her. She whispered in her ear, "If you can understand me, squeeze my hand twice."

The woman did just that! Then Cathy asked her a question that required an answer of two squeezes for yes and one for no. Through a squeeze conversation, she led the woman to the Lord!

When no one thought the woman could communicate, God showed Cathy a way. That woman died two weeks later, but I know I will see her in heaven someday.

God can use you if you trust in Him like my friend Cathy.

Praise ye the Lord. O give thanks unto the Lord;
for He is good: for His mercy endureth forever.
—Psalm 106:1

What Happened to Summer?

Summer was here, but it's gone now.
The birds are flying south.
The wild animals are on the prowl.
It's fall. I opened my mouth
To say it's too quick.
The leaves are gone from all the trees.
Today I saw the first snow fall.
Don't complain about the breeze.
Just opened my mouth in awe.
Thank God and be of good cheer.
Snuggle up in a warm blanket, cozy.
Just be happy; don't shed a tear.
Summer will come again; things will be rosy.

Chapter 21

GOD'S WAY IS BEST

Around Christmastime a few years ago, my husband was a deacon, and I was a Sunday-school teacher in our church. We also worked with the food pantry. One day, we got a call from the church secretary saying someone called and needed food.

My husband and I went to the church and sorted out some food items to take to the person that called. All we knew was that there were three people in the family.

We put the food in a van my husband used for work, which didn't have any seats in the back. We went to the address given. When we arrived, we discovered that it was the address of a small trailer. We took the food to the door and were invited inside.

As we talked to the adult present, we discovered that she was barely eighteen years old. She said her parents were in prison on drug charges, and so she was taking care of her sixteen-year-old sister and five-year-old brother.

That young lady had to take control of her family, and she was doing a marvelous job. Inside, the trailer was neat and clean.

After we delivered the food and started out the door, the five-year-old said, "Where are the presents?" Our hearts hurt for them. I don't remember what we said.

We looked around and noticed that they had a Christmas tree with nothing under it. My husband and I looked at each other, and we knew what we were thinking.

After we got into the car, we looked at each other and said, "Let's go shopping!"

It was getting late. The only store that was usually open that late was Walmart, so we found a Walmart store. I said to my husband, "I'll take the girls, and you can shop for the boy." We ran up and down the aisles looking for presents.

We also bought a big trash bag, wrapping paper, Scotch tape, ribbons, and a card.

When we got back into the van, I hopped in the back and started wrapping presents while my husband started driving back toward the little trailer home. I felt like I was on a roller-coaster ride, rolling around in the back.

By the time we got back to the trailer, I had all the packages wrapped. We put them in the trash bag, tied the top, and put a card on it saying, "Merry Christmas from Santa."

I remembered I had a big bag of clothes in the back that I was going to take to Goodwill. They would probably fit the girls!

We sneaked up on the porch and set the bags down. Then we rang the doorbell and ran back to the van and left as quickly as we could. Whew! I've always wanted to do that. (God provided the time.)

> Deliver the poor and needy; rid them
> out of the hand of the wicked.
>
> —Psalm 82:4

For This, I Am Thankful

I thank the Lord for the blessing sent my way.
I send a prayer to Him each day
For Jesus, our Savior who died for our sin.
By trusting in Him, answers He will send.
For faithful pastors who keep churches strong
As we worship God with prayer and song.
For the fruit of the land
That is nurtured and grown by His loving hand.
For answered prayers since days of old,
Safe return of a loved one dear.
Trust in God, and we won't fear.
For Christian parents that stand by the law.
I am so happy I answered His call.
Friends that come along the way,
I'm thankful and for them I do pray.
For all my family with hearts full of love,
I thank You, the All-powerful God above.

Chapter 22

GOD WANTS TO FELLOWSHIP WITH HIS CHILDREN

My husband started his own business in our home, and I was trying to be his secretary. We had some woods behind our house, and I had a special spot out there where I liked to go and pray. I longed to go there often, but the phone kept ringing and ringing. I had to answer it.

Finally, about an hour later, it stopped ringing, and I headed for the woods. Just as I reached the chair I had set out for myself, I kneeled down to pray. But the wind started to blow harder, and it began to sprinkle.

At first, I grumbled, "Oh my." Then I said, "That's okay, God. I will pray anyway."

So I started praying. I stood and looked up at the sky while I talked to Him. I walked over to the hammock and lay down.

As I relaxed, I suddenly realized that it wasn't raining anymore! I listened. There was no wind! Not even a little leaf was blowing. The only noise that touched my ears were the little birds that were singing. I started to cry. I said, "God, you want to fellowship with me enough to stop the wind and the rain so I can talk to you."

I finished talking with God then walked back to the house with a smile on my face. He really did care about visiting with me. That is the way He is with His children. Praise His holy name!

> Peace I leave with you, my peace I
> give unto you. Let not your heart be
> troubled, neither let it be afraid.
> —John 14:27

Persistence

Persistence in prayer pleases God.
He helps us wherever our feet are trod.
Something happens when we seriously pray.
He will be with you on your journey all the way.
When we look toward the sparkling stars above,
He will send you comfort along with His love.
As our prayers come from inside the heart,
He will give you a brand-new start.
Be persistent as you go.
He will be with you; your heart will know.

Chapter 23

MAMAU, IT'S IMPORTANT

My granddaughter Kylee, age six, stayed all night with me. We lay in the bed, talked a while, then I turned out the light. She scooted close to me and held my hand and lay there quiet for a while. Then she sat up and said, "Mamau, would you turn the light on?"

I asked, "Why?"

She said, "Because I have something very important to talk to you about."

I turned the light on and listened as she went on, "The other night, my brother and sister were playing a game, and I sat there watching. I put a battery in my mouth, and on accident, I swallowed it, and it has acid in it. I was laying there thinking if I would die now, I'm not saved. And I want to be so if I die, I can go to heaven. I don't know what I should do."

I told her how the Bible says we ought to pray. She fell on her face and said, "God, I know I'm a sinner. Forgive me. Now I need you to help me say it right. Jesus, would you come into my heart and save me and make me your child?"

After that, I asked her if she knew she was saved. She said, "Yes, because I asked Him to do it, and He did!" With tears in her eyes, she said, "Jesus is very special to me. And now that He is inside of me, if the battery is still there, he can just throw it out. But I believe it is out now."

> Attend unto me, and hear me: I mourn
> in my complaint and make a noise.
> —Psalm 55:2

Joy

Joy comes from the Lord.
My heart sings with praise
Because of what Jesus did.
The joy in my heart comes from the Lord
Because I have the God of love,
And I seek Him daily.
I always have hope that comes from Him.
I live with praise in my heart and joy within.
O precious is your loving-kindness,
And you are the source from which my joy comes.

Chapter 24

A DOUBLE CELEBRATION

One summer, my cousin Ron, who lived in Tennessee, was going to have his eightieth birthday. My husband and I decided to drive down to visit him on his birthday, so we drove down and got there in the afternoon of that day.

We visited for a while and celebrated his birthday. After a good meal and some birthday cake, Ron turned on the news. As we were watching, a report came on. The reporter said that the road that we had traveled on to get there had collapsed. We were shocked.

It had collapsed just a few minutes after we were on it. The damage was big enough for a car to fit in! Thankfully, a man driving a semitruck spotted it and parked there to direct traffic away from the damage. Praise God we weren't hurt!

I thought to myself, "It is a good thing that we always pray before we travel!"

> Blessed is the man that maketh
> the Lord his trust.
>
> —Psalm 40:4

God Is in the Mist

In times of grief and sadness, lift up your eyes.
He is there to comfort you as you rise.
He will put His loving arms around you.
He will always be close by to dry your eyes and hear every sigh.
He knows the thoughts and plans He has for you.
Trust in Him. He will bring you through.
He is your Shepherd. He will establish you
In every good work and word.
Every prayer directed to heaven will be heard.
You are His child, and He loves you so,
Just like your loved one is in heaven, you know.
Happy is the Lord in the death of His dear one.
Someday we will see them when we have gone on.
He has given you everlasting consolation
and good hope through grace.
So what is come to you, you will be able to face.
Remember His words in your mind.
Rejoicing, comforting, and sweetness you will find.

Chapter 25

GOD TOOK CARE OF OUR NEEDS

My husband started a heating-and-cooling business. He was installing all-new heating and cooling equipment in new homes as well as servicing them. For a few years, it was doing pretty good. Then the building market stopped. Builders stopped building. At the time, he had about thirty builders that he was depending on for work.

To keep afloat, he had to reform the business and change it to just servicing and installing equipment in existing homes. That meant he had to let all the men go. It was just him and our son. Now all the bills had to be paid, and we had to start all over again. We had to sell all the property we owned in another state, and it almost wiped out our savings.

To keep ourselves moving and trusting, we went to our church's gym in the evenings several times a week. We walked at least two miles in the gym every time. Then we would go to the altar and pray. What were we going to do? We didn't tell anyone but God about how bad it was and just kept trusting.

Christmas was coming up, and our house payment was due. We had no money to give to keep our house, and we especially didn't have any for presents.

One night, while we were walking, our pastor stopped by the church. We didn't know he was there, and we hadn't told him our problem. But when we started to leave, he walked over to us and handed us a check for a thousand dollars! We were astounded!

It paid for our house payment and for some Christmas presents for our family. After that, I can't even tell you how, but God worked it out, and the business got us through.

> Many, O Lord our God, are thy wonderful
> works which thou hast done and thy thoughts
> are to us-ward that cannot be reckoned up in
> order unto thee. If I would declare and speak of
> them. They are more than can be numbered.
> —Psalm 40:5

The Cross

As I look at a memorial cross:

It reminds me of a loved one that gave his life
for our freedom in the war.
Also, it reminds me of Jesus and the pain he
bore.
He did it to set us free from the power of sin.
He is waiting for you to let him come in.
The door is open; ask him today.
Believe in your heart and start to pray.
You may be sad and feel like it's made of stone.
He wants you to ask him in so you can be his
own.
He is waiting for you to surrender your heart out
of pure love
Because the Holy Spirit comes from the Father
above.

Chapter 26

I'M NOT SICK

My mother had just been told that she had breast cancer. One day, my mother came home from the doctor after having surgery. She had just had a lump removed from her breast.

She came home and never went to bed. I said, "Mother, shouldn't you be in bed? You just had surgery."

She said, "Why? I'm not sick." So she didn't go to bed until that evening.

A week or two later, she went back for a checkup, and the doctor said she was full of cancer and only had a few months to live. But Mother kept saying, "Those doctors keep saying I'm sick, but I'm not. I have a God who can take care of me."

About a month later, Mother went back for a checkup to see what they could do. Believe it or not, she was cancer-free. She was seventy years old. She lived to be eighty-two, and she didn't die of cancer. She died of heart failure in her sleep.

Oh, sing to the LORD a new song!
For he has done marvelous things.
—Psalm 98:1

Life

As we go through life, don't look back.
Looking back, you will see hurt, pain, sorrow,
   and regret.
Keep moving forward!
Looking back is for time travelers.
Looking forward is where you find peace, love,
   and joy.
Trust in the Lord with all your heart and lean not
   unto your own understanding.
In all your ways, acknowledge Him, and He will
   direct your path.
Trusting God will bring miracles into your life.
Look forward to serving Him and waiting on His
   answers as we travel through life on earth.
Look up as age creeps up on you, for He is pre-
   paring a place for you eternally.
You're not there, yes. So keep looking forward
   until that day comes.

Chapter 27

THE SILVER BRIDGE

The Silver Bridge was a bridge in Point Pleasant, West Virginia, that crossed over to Ohio. My in-laws owned chickens, and every week, I would take my mother-in-law across the bridge, north of Point Pleasant, to sell eggs to a store in Ohio. (I was living with my husband's parents in West Virginia when he was stationed in Vietnam.)

One day, I got up and came downstairs, and my mother-in-law said, "I don't feel well, so I'm not going to sell eggs this morning."

I said, "I'm sorry you don't feel well, but I think I will just go to Point Pleasant to visit a friend whose husband is also serving in Vietnam."

So I went to visit that friend. And while I was at her house, the lights flickered, and we heard a loud noise. We looked at each other and thought, "Don't tell me the Vietcong are here!" We jumped again a few minutes later.

A few minutes later, someone came to the back door and said that the Silver Bridge had fallen in. Lots of people were on it and many drowned. If we had gone over the bridge to sell eggs that day, we would have also fallen. Bless the Lord, O my soul, for saving us from trouble!

> Our help is in the name of the Lord,
> who made heaven and earth.
> —Psalm 124:8

Our God Is an Awesome God

He made the heavens, the earth, and the sky.
He made the flowers and the trees.
He made you and I.
He made the birds and the bees.
We should praise Him every day.
He put the stars in the sky to shine.
Get down on your knees and pray.
He sent Jesus to die on the cross for your soul
    and mine.
Yes, an awesome God is He.
He came to the earth as a man.
He went to the cross to set us free.
For our God, we should stand.
Hallelujah, an awesome God is He!

Chapter 28

MY PRAYER TREE

When I was a kid growing up, I was a real tomboy and loved to climb trees. I grew up by a river and loved to pray while looking over the water. In our backyard now, we have an acre of woods. Lloyd, being the husband he is, dug a pond and had a bridge built out at the edge of the woods so that I would have a nice place to go and pray.

One day when I was sixty, I went out to talk to the Lord as always. The mosquitos were so bad that I could not stay very long. Frustrated, I looked up into the tree and said, "Lord, how high do mosquitos fly?"

So I climbed the tree by the pond, and I found out if I climbed high enough, the mosquitos did not bother me. That summer, I made that higher spot in the tree my prayer spot.

The next summer, most of the trees had been hit by ash borers, including my prayer tree, so I could not climb it anymore. As I was heading outside one day, I saw a black cloud in the sky. It was coming toward our house. I stepped back inside to watch and see what it was. Then all of a sudden, our whole backyard was full of dragonflies. They were swooping down and eating the mosquitos as they came out of the ground.

My husband had been on the mower and was batting the dragonflies. I yelled out, "Don't bother them! They are our friends. God sent them to get rid of the mosquitos!" They were there for about half an hour, and then they were gone.

For a few years, our backyard was mosquito-free.

> O God, my heart is fixed; I will sing
> and give praise, even with my glory.
> —Psalm 108:1

{ *Katie's Song* }

My granddaughter Katie, at four years old, came to me one day and said, "Mammy, I wrote you a song." I listened to it and wrote it down so I could remember it.

"I Love You, Lord"

I thank you, Lord, for sending me my Mammy
And that you made her a disciple.
I want to be a disciple like her.
I love you, Lord.
I love you, Lord. I love you, Lord,
For dying on the cross for me and raise
again. So I can be with you.
I love you, Lord. I love you, Lord.
I love you, Lord.

Chapter 29

NOT BY CHANCE

There was a lady that came to our church from another religion. (I didn't know this at the time.)

After she had come to our church a few times, I saw her in a grocery store. I greeted her and asked, "How do you like our church?"

She said, "I do like it. Everyone is so friendly." She mentioned that people in the church she went to before weren't so nice.

I asked her, "Are you saved?"

She said, "I don't know what that means."

I explained to her how God sent His Son to earth to die on the cross to bear our sins upon Himself. I explained how, after God created Adam and Eve, they fell into the sin of disobedience, and that caused everyone that was born after to be born into sin.

So God sent his Son to earth to take our sins away if we would accept Him as our Savior.

We talked for a few minutes, and she said, "I want to do that."

She prayed and was gloriously saved! She went home and told her mother (to whom she didn't speak English) what she had done, and she led her to the Lord.

The Lord prepared two souls for His kingdom that day.

From the end of the earth I will cry unto
thee, when my heart is overwhelmed. Lead
me to the rock that is higher than I.
—Psalm 61:1

My Christmas Tree
It Is Trimmed to Represent the
Real Meaning of Christmas

Look at the way it is shaped; it points up toward heaven to glorify the Father in heaven. The star stands for the Christ Child that was born on Christmas Day.

It is an evergreen because we will live forever in heaven if we know Him as our Savior.

I call the tree Jesus's birthday cake with all the lights, which are like the candles on our birthday cakes. It also shows us that He is the Light of the World.

On the tree, I put roses because He is the Rose of Sharon. The red ones represent the blood He shed on Calvary for my sins.

I put on white bows to show that though my sins may be as scarlet, he washes me white as snow.

The green on the tree reminds us that we grow in grace every day.

It holds, on the top, angels playing instruments, praising the Lord as they do in heaven.

As you look around the tree, you will see ornaments that were given to me by my friends. It brings back memories of past and present friendships that God has blessed me with.

It has one rope of gold beads that wind up the
      tree, which reminds me of the streets of gold
      where some of my loved ones are with Jesus.
The presents under the tree are my gifts to loved
      ones that show my love here on earth. Inside
      are treasures I picked to show my love for
      them.
The tree is never worshiped or treasured; it's just
      a symbol. On the other side of the room,
      the Christmas story is read to the children
      at Christmastime.
Because the real gift that was given on Christmas
      Day was wrapped in swaddling clothes and
      laid in a manger—Jesus.

Chapter 30

MY DADDY'S HEALING

My dad smoked for forty years and ended up with emphysema. And later, he developed cancer in his sixties.

The doctor told him he would have to have one lung taken out and part of the other.

We prayed for him, and when the doctor took him in for surgery, they found that one lung was healed and part of the other was taken out. But that is not the end of the story.

When Dad was eighty-two in 1998, my husband and I went to see my parents. When we got there, my mom called 911 because my dad couldn't breathe. He said to me, "I won't make it back this time."

I said to him, "If you don't, do you know where you are going?"

His response was "No, and I'm afraid to die."

I was beside myself. I thought he was saved.

So I hopped up on the bed and started talking. I told him how to get saved. He said the sinner's prayer, and I asked him if he knew he was saved now. He said, "I don't believe God can forgive me for the things I've done in my life."

I asked him what he thought God would not forgive him for, not that I wanted to know. I just told him that when we confess our sins and ask God to forgive us, He throws them as far as the east is from the west and buries them at the bottom of the sea and remembers them no more (Micah 7:19).

I told him to just trust God for that. "Throw your hands in the air as a sign that you are giving it all to God, and trust what His Word says."

He did that and started to cry.

I said, "Do you know you are saved now?"

He said yes.

I said, "Praise the Lord."

He went to the hospital. The next day, the doctor said he would live about three days, go into a coma, and die.

My husband and another lady were in the room with him. We started singing and praising God.

We went back the next day. He was asleep, but we still sang in his room.

On the third day, we went back, and he was sitting up eating breakfast.

He came home. That was January 1998. His family doctor asked what they did to him in the hospital to make him breathe better. He said it wasn't the doctors; it was God.

I had been asking God for two more years for my dad to live for a reason.

That was in January 1998, and in January 2000, he went to be with the Lord. Now he is healed forever (Psalm 103:2–4).

Insight

The Bible says there is a time for everything.
In my years of life, I've found that that is true.
We live and we die, and we get money, and we
    lose it all.
We have love and lose it too.
All we can do is trust God in all things.
Whatever comes will go,
But God will be with us through it all.
Rich, poor, sick, or well—He will be there to
    help us through it all, come what may.
God is our provider.
Put your trust in Him to conquer whatever
    comes.

Chapter 31

THE COFFEEHOUSE

A few years ago, my husband, a friend, and I decided to meet at a coffee shop for a Bible study. We met there every Thursday. After we had been meeting there for a while, the workers started to ask us what we were doing. We told them that we were studying the Bible. Sometimes we would order food as well as coffee to be polite.

Gradually, the workers would ask us questions about the Bible. When the coffeehouse had closed, the workers would lock the doors but let us stay because they had a drive-through that closed later.

Sometimes I would sketch pictures while sitting there, and as customers came in, they would see my work and ask questions. I asked some of them if they wanted me to do a sketch of them. Some said yes, and so, while I was drawing a sketch of that person, I witnessed to them. I would tell them where I got my talent (from God, of course) because that was when God let me know that He gave me that talent to be able to tell others how I got saved.

After a while, we were able to lead four of the workers to the Lord, but the most exciting one was when my husband got to know a young man named Joe. He was Vietnamese, and his family were Buddhists. My husband asked him if he could tell him anything about a man called Jesus. Joe told him that he was a teacher from long ago, and my husband told him about Apostle Paul. Paul fell to his knees when God spoke to him on the road to the city of Damascus. Paul saw the light of God, and he was blinded. Paul had been killing Christians, thinking he was right, but Jesus appeared to him and told him he was wrong.

Joe said he had been looking for that light. He confessed that he had been drinking and driving and had a car accident in which his best friend was killed. That day, Joe saw the light that he had been looking for.

So my husband told him what it was all about, that Jesus was that light. And in the process, he led Joe to the Lord. He was happy he found the light. Then he wondered, "What am I going to tell my family now that I'm a Christian?"

We didn't see him again until about a year later. He was in college and serving God. We never asked him what he told his family, but we know God worked it out.

> That was the true light, which lighteth
> every man that cometh into the world.
> —John 1:9

God's Beauty

The white snow on the mountains
The water falling like nature's fountains
The birds flying high in the sky
I can't describe it—no need to try.
The beauty God created to enjoy
My mind is not big enough to employ.
The grace that God has given us
Enjoy it today, don't throw a fuss.
Praise Him for His beauty today.
Bow down to our wonderful God and pray.

Chapter 32

FLAT TIRE

Me and my sisters, Anna and Sue, were going to see our parents in West Virginia. As we travelled along on an isolated West Virginia road, we heard a *boom*! Oh no! It was a flat tire.

I got out, opened the trunk, got a tool, and carried it over to the tire. As I was approaching the tire, all of a sudden, a man in a truck jumped out and grabbed the tool. Off came the bolts. Then he went to the trunk, picked up the tire, and just like a robot, put the tire on without a word. I hardly had time to say thank you. He grunted and jumped back in the truck and was gone.

I often wondered, was he a man or an angel?

Is Our Basket Full?

At a ladies' meeting at church, I asked the Lord to
give me ideas for decorating a special kind
of wedding.
"The Bride of Christ"—that is when Jesus comes
to take Christians to be His bride.
I used a basket to represent us Christians as His
bride.
It was filled with fruit to represent the souls we
have won to Christ.
As Christians, have we won a soul lately?
Do we have a burden for those who are lost?
Will our basket be full, or will it be empty?
Do we care? Do we have that burden?
Ask God to give you that burden so we can fill
that basket.
How will we feel when Jesus comes to take us
home?
He might come soon.

Chapter 33

A Car on Fire

When my husband was away in the military, I was driving on a country road with an older lady riding in the car. Suddenly, I couldn't believe my eyes! There were flames coming from underneath the hood of the car. I said, "Fire!" And then I pulled into a gravel area.

The lady and I jumped out just in time to see a tow truck stopping to help. He put the fire out and told us to get into the truck. He towed the car to the nearest tow station and repair shop.

Then the man took us back to where I was living at the time. I said, "Thank you so much!"

We never saw him again. But whoever he was, he was sent by God.

> Be pleased, O Lord, to deliver me:
> O Lord, make haste to help me.
> —Psalm 40:13

What Would Be?

What would be?
If my heart didn't sing,
What would be if the church bells didn't ring?
If I were discouraged,
What would be if I wasn't encouraged?
If I would just give up today,
What would be if I didn't pray?
I'm so glad that I do sing.
I'm so glad the church bells ring.
I'm not discouraged; Jesus is there.
I can talk to Him in prayer.

Chapter 34

THE LOST KEY

It was beginning to get dark outside when a friend of mine called me and said she had lost the keys to her house. She was outdoors raking leaves and had lost them somewhere. My husband and I grabbed our flashlights and went over to help her. The first thing we did was have prayer. Then we started the search.

The leaves in her backyard were about three feet high. She had raked all of them to the end of her yard. We looked in the front yard, but there was no sign of the keys. We looked at the side of the house and still no sign. Then we started at the back door and went out from there. Finally, we got to the pile of leaves that was running across the back of the yard. It was positively impossible to try to find them in there. It was dark by now, but with God, all things are possible.

We started looking in the leaves that were piled up, and after about half an hour, we got to the edge of the yard by a tree. My husband and Ella were raking leaves here and there. I walked over by a tree and saw something shining through the leaves. I said, "What is that?"

My husband lifted away some leaves, and there they were. It was the last place we looked.

We praised the Lord that we found the keys.

God Created It All

As I look up to the sky, I see the stars that twinkle,
The moon shines a soft golden glow.
I ponder the beauty as I look to and fro,
As I look to the snowcapped mountains and to the rugged hills.
God's creation is so great; it fills my heart with thrills.
I look to the earth, oceans, rivers, and seas.
As I admire the beauty, it does appear, a soft spring breeze.
I look to the ground; I see flowers and trees.
The woods are full of animals as they go wending along.
God made it all, and it made me sing a song.
Man was made in God's own image in the Bible;
it is known.
God created man with a soul to be his very own.

Chapter 35

EASTER PAGEANT

The Easter pageant was next week, and I still had invitations to pass out. So I grabbed my coat because it looked like rain. As I stepped out the door, it started to sprinkle. I said, "Okay, God. I'll go ahead and do it in the rain because it's important."

Our house was two hundred feet from the road, and when I got to the road, it wasn't raining anymore. As I walked past my neighbors, I heard a noise. It was rain pouring on their house about one hundred feet from the road! I walked along the road and put the invitations in the boxes. I looked at every house. Rain was pouring down their roofs.

I walked all the way to the end of the road, and the rain never got any closer to me than one hundred feet. I walked back to my house after I had delivered all the invitations. Not one drop of rain hit me all the way down and back. As I entered the back of my house, it started to pour.

> I will delight myself in thy statutes:
> I will not forget thy word.
> —Psalm 119:16

Rockaby baby in a sailboat
When the wind blows, they will start to float.
Mommy, Daddy, and Baby makes three
While little sisters are home having tea.
As the waves come, the boat will rock.
Baby will fall asleep in the deep blue sea.
Daddy is so proud as he starts to talk.
Mommy will touch baby's cheek, soft as a cloud.
Baby will start to cry really loud!
Mommy says, "Time to go home. It is the end.
"But what a day we did spend.
"The fish are jumping out of the water high
"As we fix our eyes on the color of the sky.
"The sunset is overwhelming, I see.
"It's so overwhelming to me.
"Let's do this again some other day."
Her heart did melt as Daddy started to pray.
"God bless our little ones as they grow.
"May their feet walk where God guides them to and fro."

Chapter 36

SAVED BY GRACE

There was a young man named Matthew who came to work for my son's business. One day, he got out of his car outside the office, and I asked him if he knew Jesus as his Savior. He said, "I'm working on it." I told him about creation and about how God made Adam and Eve in the beautiful garden and how sin had caused them to be kicked out of the garden. Now they had to die someday because of their disobedience. They were made to live forever with God, but sin had changed all that. Now blood had to be shed in order to get to heaven.

That was when God sent His Son (Jesus) down to earth to die and to shed His sinless blood on the cross for us. Only if we accept His Son as our Savior can we be saved and live in heaven with God forever.

After that, I kept praying that God would convict his heart. I gave him a book of miracles to read.

A while after that, I was in the office, and he said, "I want you to be the first to know that I accepted Jesus as my Savior."

I started to cry. I was so blessed. Thank you, Lord, for saving one more soul.

> To see thy power and thy glory, so I
> have seen thee in the sanctuary.
> —Psalm 63:2

Look Up

No matter where you are, you can always look up.
You might be in danger, running from a stranger.
    Look up.
Living in sin, don't know where to begin. Look up.
You can be flying in an airplane or think you are
    going insane. Look up.
Doesn't matter where you are, driving in a car.
Look up to God. He is always there in heaven.
Ask Him to forgive your sin.
He will make your life worthwhile.
He can even put on your face a smile.
So look up today and let God have His way.
Fall down on your knees and pray.
You won't be sorry; He will take away your worry.

Chapter 37

SHE WANTED TO KNOW

Her name was Ruth. She had been a friend of mine for a while, but she was caught up in a marriage that wasn't going well. Her husband owned a sinful business and wasn't faithful. He wanted her to work for him, but she didn't want to.

One day, I was at her house. I told her about Jesus and what He did for her. A few days later, she called me and said, "Would you come over to my house and tell me more about this getting-saved thing?"

I was welcomed in, and I spoke to her about what the Bible says about salvation and how she could be saved from that awful place called hell. She listened to everything I said and read from the Word. Then she accepted Jesus as her Savior.

What I didn't know was that her son was listening in the other room. He walked in and said, "I want to know Jesus too." So that day, God provided two souls for His kingdom. Praise His holy name!

She left her husband and moved away. I did not see her for a quite a while. Then one day, while I was out shopping, I saw her. I was happily told that she had met a Christian man, and they were married and were living in another state.

From Boy to Man

There was little boy as cute as can be.
We would play in the yard and even climb a tree.
He had blond hair and sang a song to me.
I will never forget the times we had, so lively and
free.
Now that boy is grown as handsome, so you see.
Time to start another life with a wife very
patiently.
Grandson, I'm proud of you, the man you have
become. For He,
Jesus, died on the cross for you and me.
Trust in Him with all your heart for a happy
family.
Someday you will be with Him because of
Calvary.

Chapter 38

GOD HEARD ME

While I was staying with my husband's parents in West Virginia, my husband's uncle died. It had rained a lot that morning on the graveled old country road. I went to town to buy something to wear for the funeral. On the way back home, I was in a hurry so I wouldn't be late for the funeral. I was driving on a crooked country road a little too fast, and all of a sudden, the car started slipping and sliding all over the road. I tried to keep it under control. There was a slip in the road above a hill from which I was driving. The right tire hit the slip that was shaped like a V. In that moment, I said, "God, help me."

I didn't do a thing, but my foot hit the gas pedal. All of a sudden, the car was stopped, buried in mud on the other side of the road next to the hill. I don't know how I got there because I don't remember anything until the car was stopped.

I got out of the car to look at the situation. Then I got back in and tried to move it, but it was very stuck in the mud. I knew I couldn't get it out myself.

I looked up, and the mailman was coming up the road. He looked at the problem, looked at me, and said, "You are a lucky girl." His cousin had told him that the farmer across the creek from the store had a tractor.

So I called Farmer Stuart, and he sent one of his sons to pull me out of the mud. I went out by the road, and when I saw the tractor coming, he stopped and didn't say a word. I got on. I started to think, *Is this one of the Stuart boys?* I said to him, "Are you one of the Stuart boys?"

He grinned and said, "Yes."

We arrived at the spot where my car was stuck in the mud. He laughed and said, "Your car is buried." He got out a chain and hooked it to the car. He was able to pull it out.

It was a white car, so I had to go meet everyone in a polka-dot car. It had mud all over it. I rode with my husband's cousins in the funeral procession.

God saved my life that day with a short prayer: "God, help me." He heard me and answered my prayer.

> Blessed be the name of the Lord from
> this time forth and forevermore.
> —Psalm 113:2

Chapter 39

MY COUSIN HENRY

I grew up on a farm in West Virginia. It was the same farm my cousin did. His name was Henry. He didn't go to church and was always into mischief.

When we were grown up, I saw him at a family reunion. We were overlooking our relatives in the ball diamond below, which had been turned into a playground for the children. As we stood there looking, I said, "I wonder how many people came this year. But on second thought, I wonder how many saved people are here." I looked over at him and asked, "Do you know Jesus as your Savior?"

He said, "No! I know where I am going, and I will have a lot of company when I get there."

After that conversation, I stopped talking and started praying.

A few weeks went by, and I decided to write him a letter in love. I told him how God loved him and a few things the Bible said about salvation. His wife said that he read the letter, threw it on the floor, picked it up, and read it again. And then he cursed me.

A few weeks went by, and the Lord burdened my heart to send him a card with a note. It just said, "I love you, and I am praying for you."

I did this for I don't know how long. Then, on Christmas, I bought him a Bible. I gave it to my mother because he came to see her often, and I was living far away at the time. When she gave it to him, he said, "That is a good gift." It surprised us both!

The next time I saw him was at my brother's funeral. He had been electrocuted on his job and died immediately. Thank the Lord, he was a Christian!

As Henry walked through the door of the funeral home, instead of his usual indifference or anger toward me, he gave me a hug.

I kept the notes going to his house. Then a few years later, his dad died. I went to the funeral and saw him at the casket. He said bluntly, "I know where he went." I didn't say a word, but he continued, "Dad reached up and said, 'My little Molly and Polly!' And he died." (Those he mentioned were his younger twin sisters that had passed away as babies.)

I prayed for him for eighteen years and sent him cards. Then one day, my mother said he had stomach cancer. I told my husband we had to go see him. He agreed.

The next day, Saturday, we drove to West Virginia. We went into his house, and my husband was able to lead him to the Lord. He cried like a baby, and so did his wife and daughters, who were already Christians.

I thank God for His loving-kindness.

> Clap your hands, all ye people: shout
> unto God with the voice of triumph.
>
> —Psalm 47:1

Chapter 40

OKAY, I'LL PRAY

I watched my great-grandson one day a week. And every day I watched him, we would read a Bible story, and then we would pray. When he was three years old, after our story time, I said, "Well, it's time to pray now."

He said, "Nope."

I said, "You don't want to pray?"

He said, "Nope."

I said, "You don't want to talk to God?"

He said, "Nope."

I said to him, "Come with me for a minute."

We went to the living room, and I stood him in the window seat and said, "Look up into the sky. That is where God lives. Look at the trees and the grass. God made all of that plus all of the animals and everything. He made you and me too. He sent His Son down to earth to die on the cross so we can go to heaven someday."

He said, "Okay, I'll pray."

> His seed shall be mighty upon earth: the
> generation of the upright shall be blessed.
> —Psalm 112:2

Looking to Christmas

When we look forward to Christmas every year, we don't just celebrate the birth of a baby.

After living in heaven as God's only Son, Jesus—with all the glory of heaven—chose to leave heaven for us.

It is celebrating that God loved us so much that He sent His Son to earth to be born as a man, to grow up in this wicked world, to die on the cross, and to take the sins of all mankind upon Himself. He rose from the grave on Easter (Resurrection Day) and went back to heaven to be with God. He said to the disciples, "Where I go, you will be also." That means if we ask forgiveness for our sins and invite Jesus into our hearts, part of God (the Holy Spirit) comes to live inside of us, and we are adopted into the family of God.

The Bible says in John 14:16, "And I will pray the Father, and He shall give you another Comforter, that He may abide with you forever." And John 14:6 states, "Jesus said unto him, I am the Way, the Truth, and the Life; no man cometh unto the Father but by me."

So this Christmas, let's celebrate why Jesus came to earth.

About the Author

Mary L. accepted Jesus as her Savior at the age of twenty-two in 1967. At that time, her husband was in the Vietnam War. That same year, she discovered God had given her a talent to paint and glorify her Father in heaven. A few years later, she joined an art guild and sold her paintings. She spent her life decorating to make things pretty for weddings and parties at church. She taught Sunday school for children for fifty years and was also active in ladies' ministries.